# The Coloring Book of Urban Sketches

## 101 Cities & Scenes

**NORTH LIGHT BOOKS**
CINCINNATI, OHIO
ARTISTSNETWORK.COM

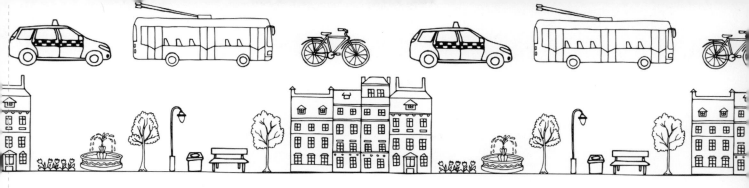

# Introduction

I'll admit it. **I am a city person.** And I'm guessing you and I may have this in common. There's little I enjoy more than being on foot in a city—any city will do, as each has it's own unique personality—and just exploring. Skyscrapers and brownstones. Pocket parks and bustling metro centers. Hip cafés and famous landmarks. Historic architecture and gleaming new construction. I can and often do walk for miles. And miles. And some more miles. Some of my favorite places to walk and sightsee are Paris and Chicago, Portland and Dublin, and San Francisco and London. But there are far more places I'd like to visit than I've actually been to and many more that I'm sure I haven't even thought of yet.

And that's where **The Coloring Book of Urban Sketches** comes in. Within these pages you will find 101 of the best and most diverse scenes I could find, all hand-rendered and ready to color, a fantasyland of the places I dream of visiting. Some of the scenes are of real places and some are only imagined. Some are loose and sketchy, others tight and measured. You'll find seamless repeating patterns as well as scenes that are free and easy.

I hope what you'll ultimately find is a few minutes or hours of solace, of relaxation, of meditation. Pick up some markers or colored pencils (or even crayons or watercolors), and lose yourself in coloring in these scenes. I'm eager and curious to see your interpretations of these lovingly selected illustrations, and I invite you to share your pages via Facebook, Instagram and Twitter—just tag your photos and videos with **#cbofurbansketches** and have a great time!

**~Kristy Conlin**

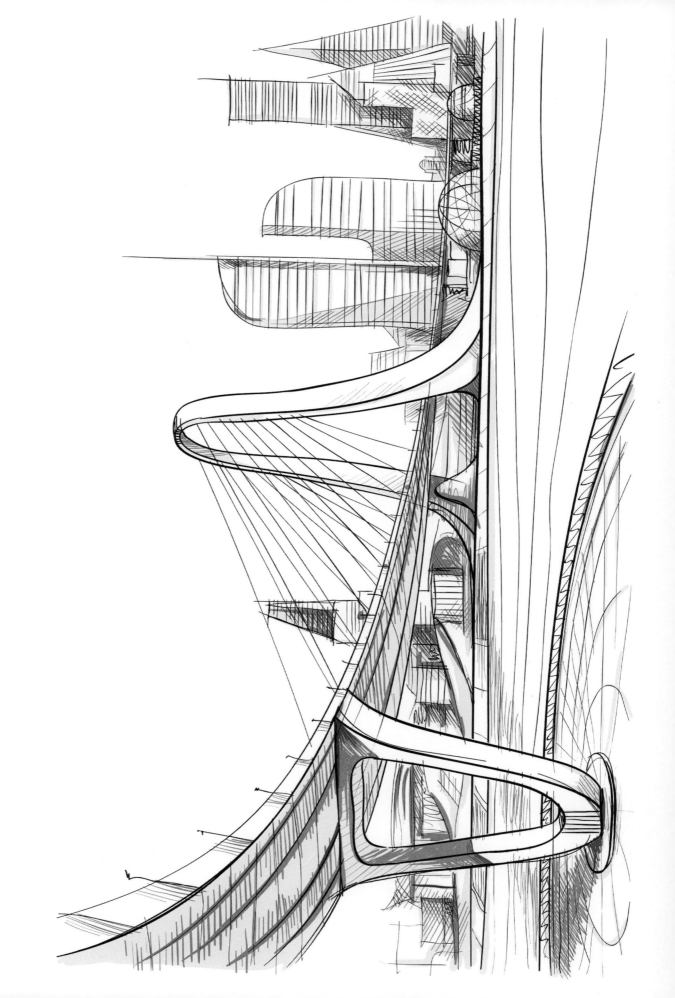

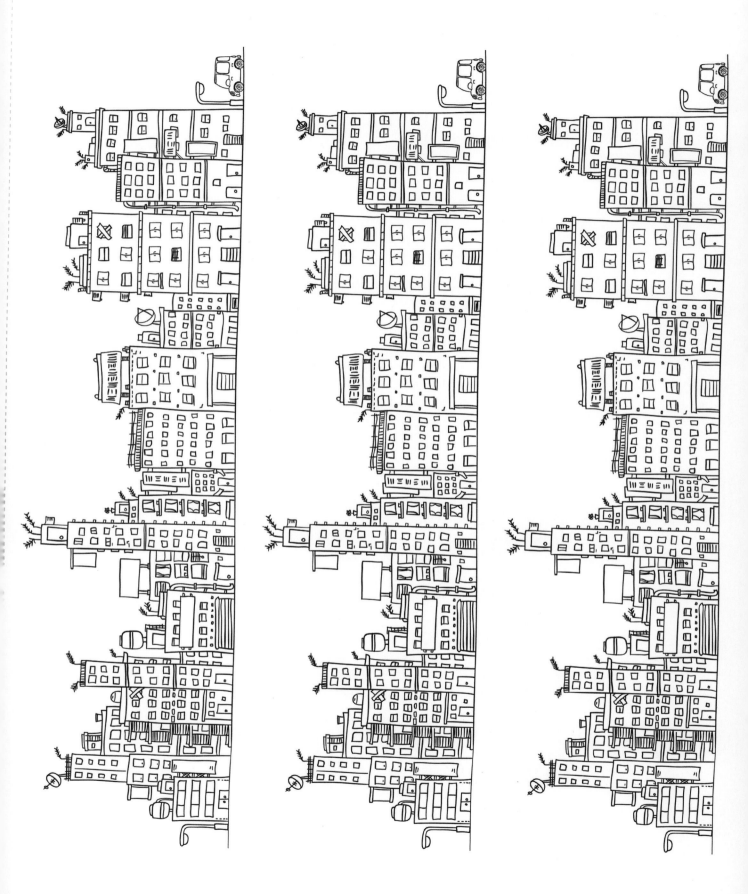

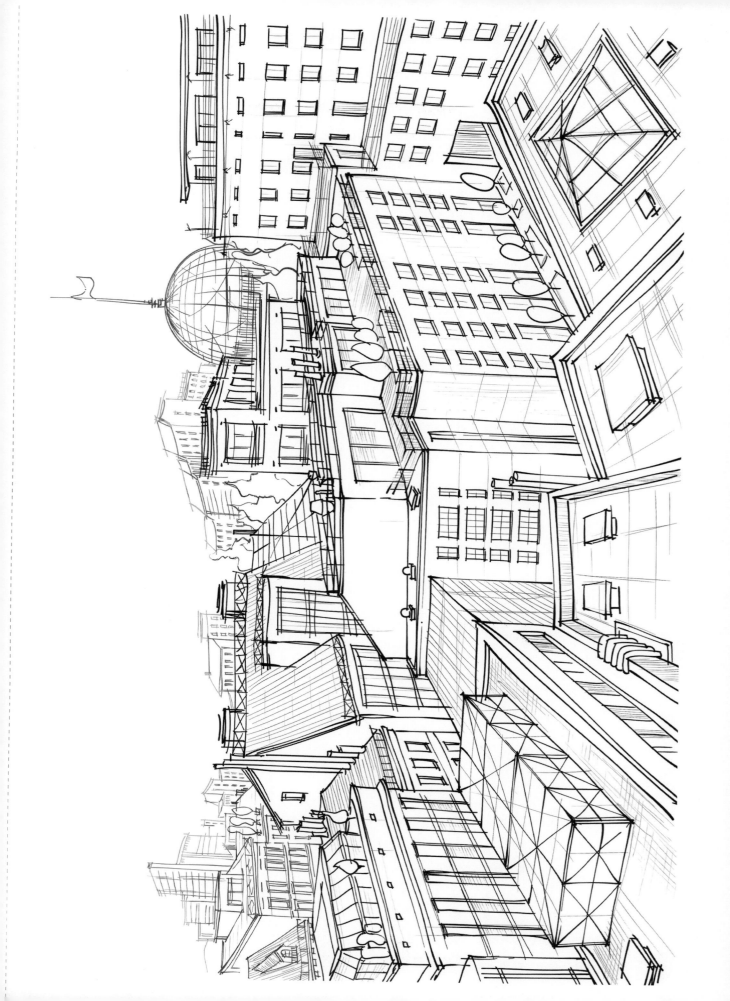

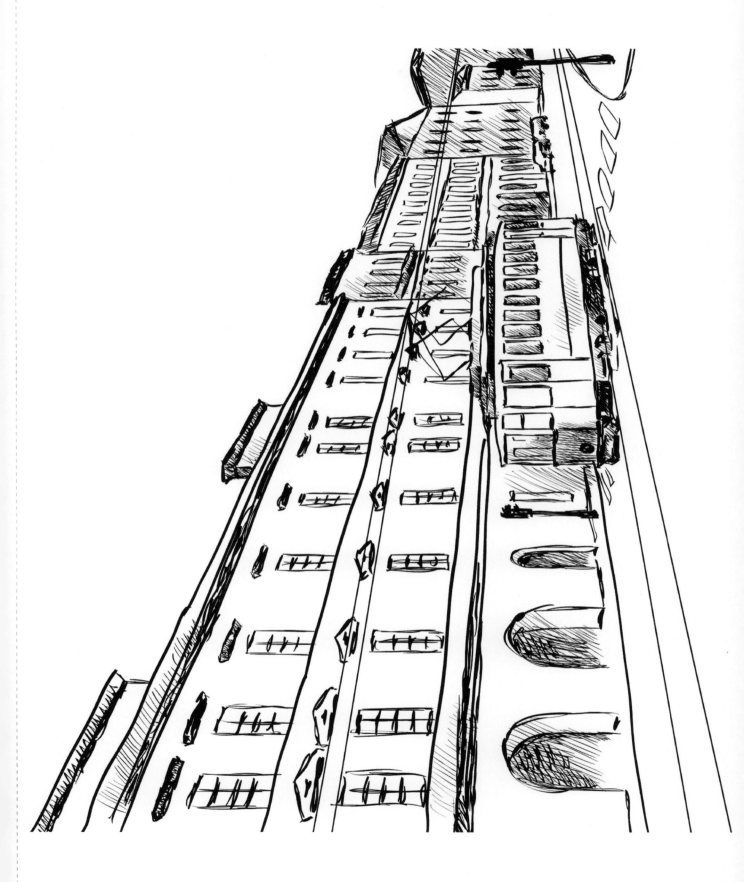

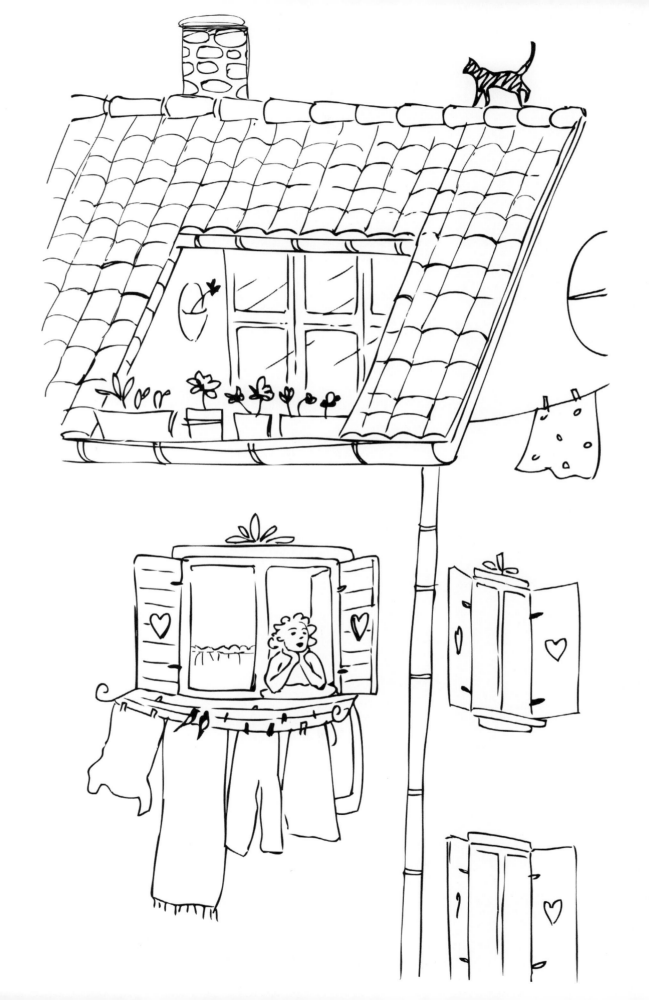

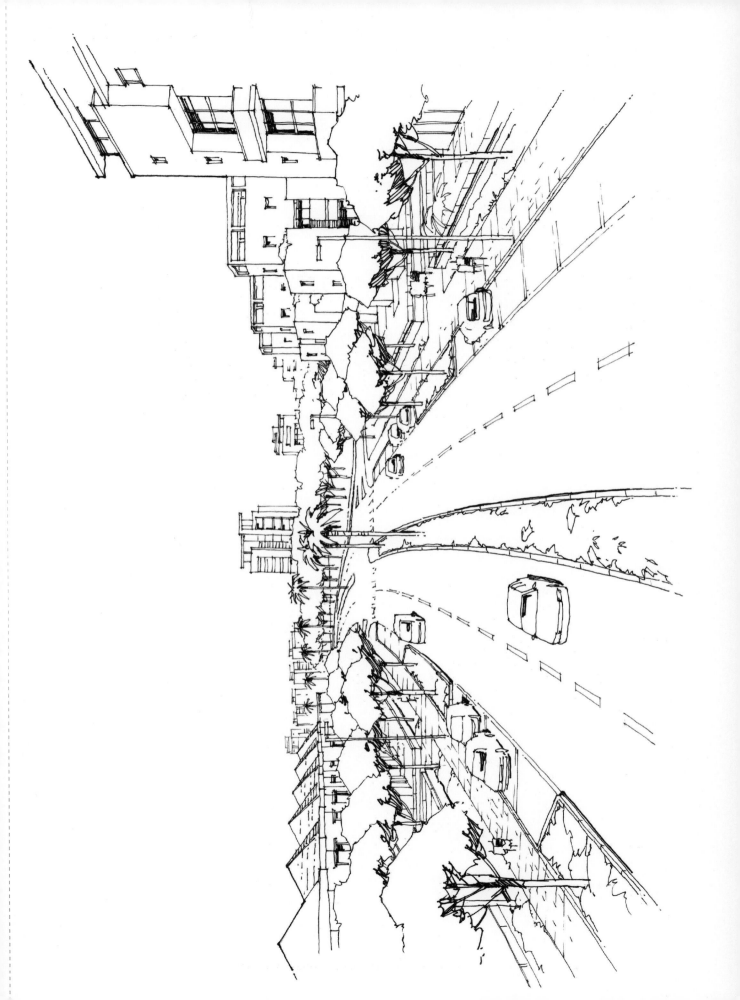

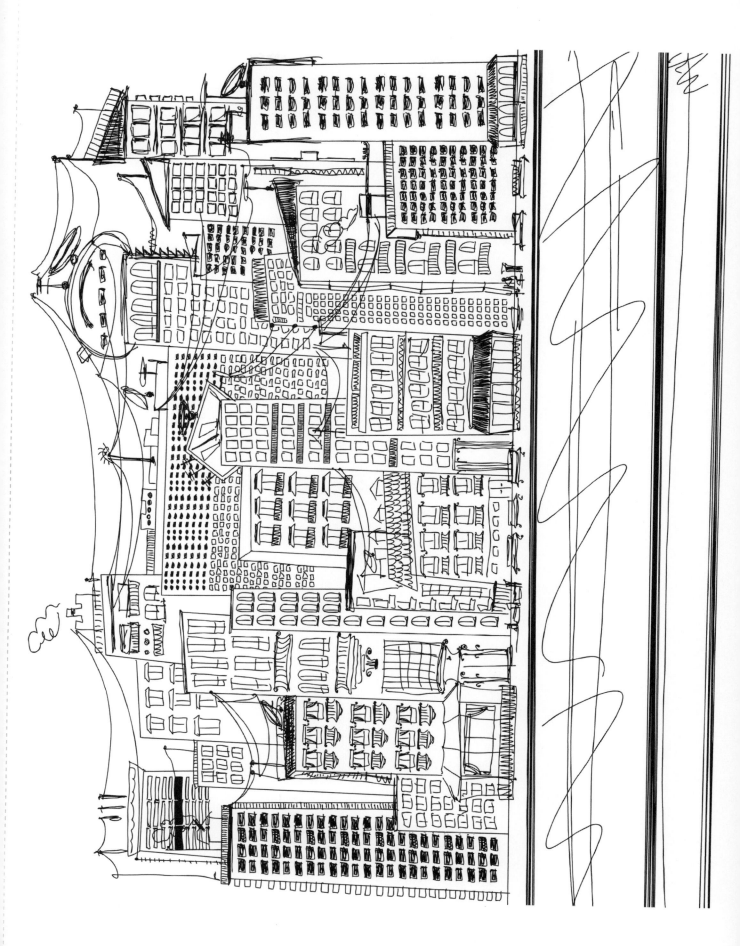

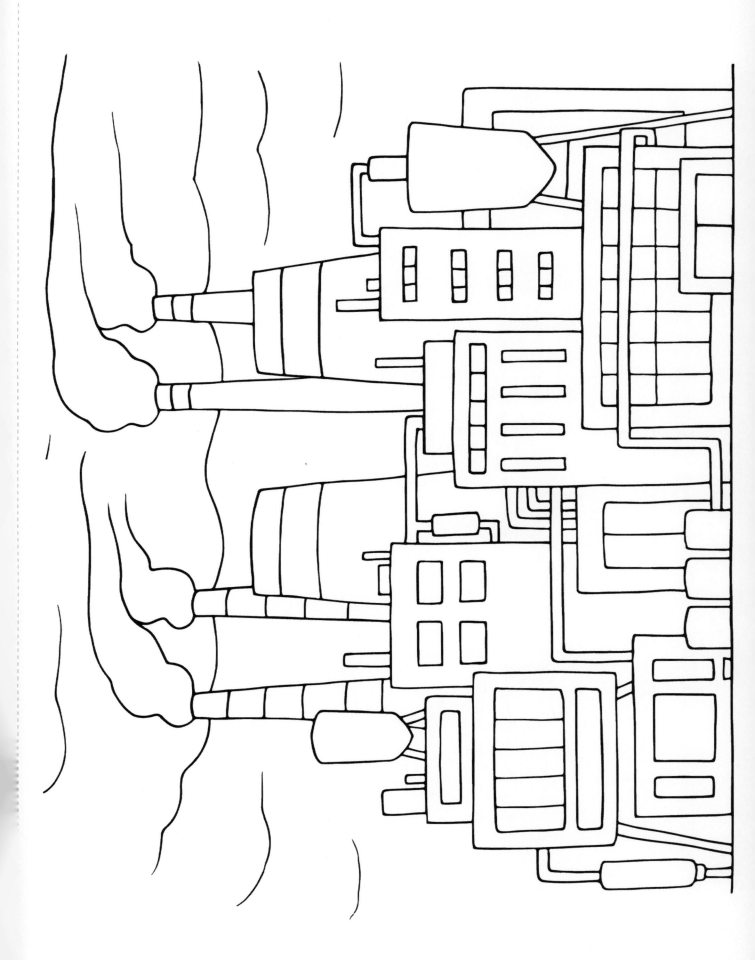

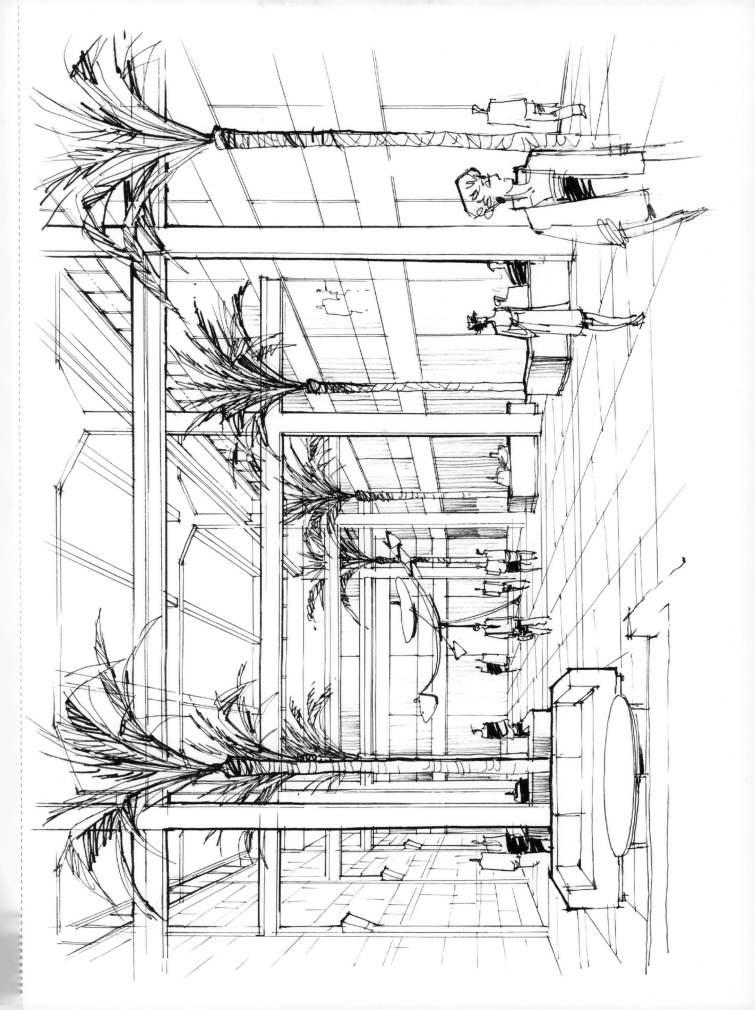

Lisbon

SEOUL
KOREAN TRADITIONAL HOUSES

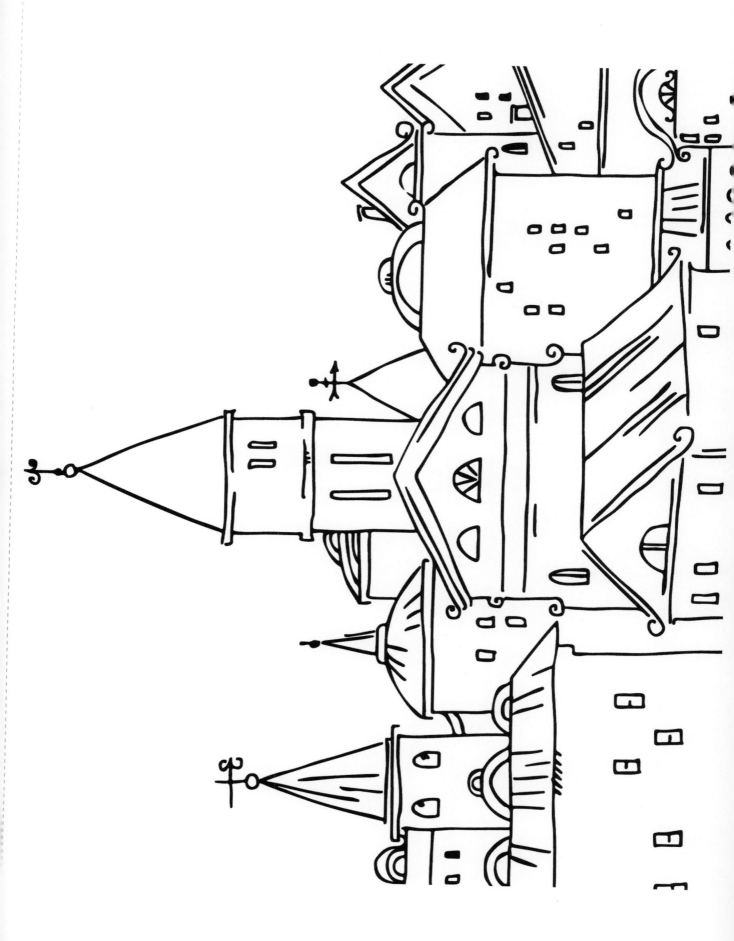

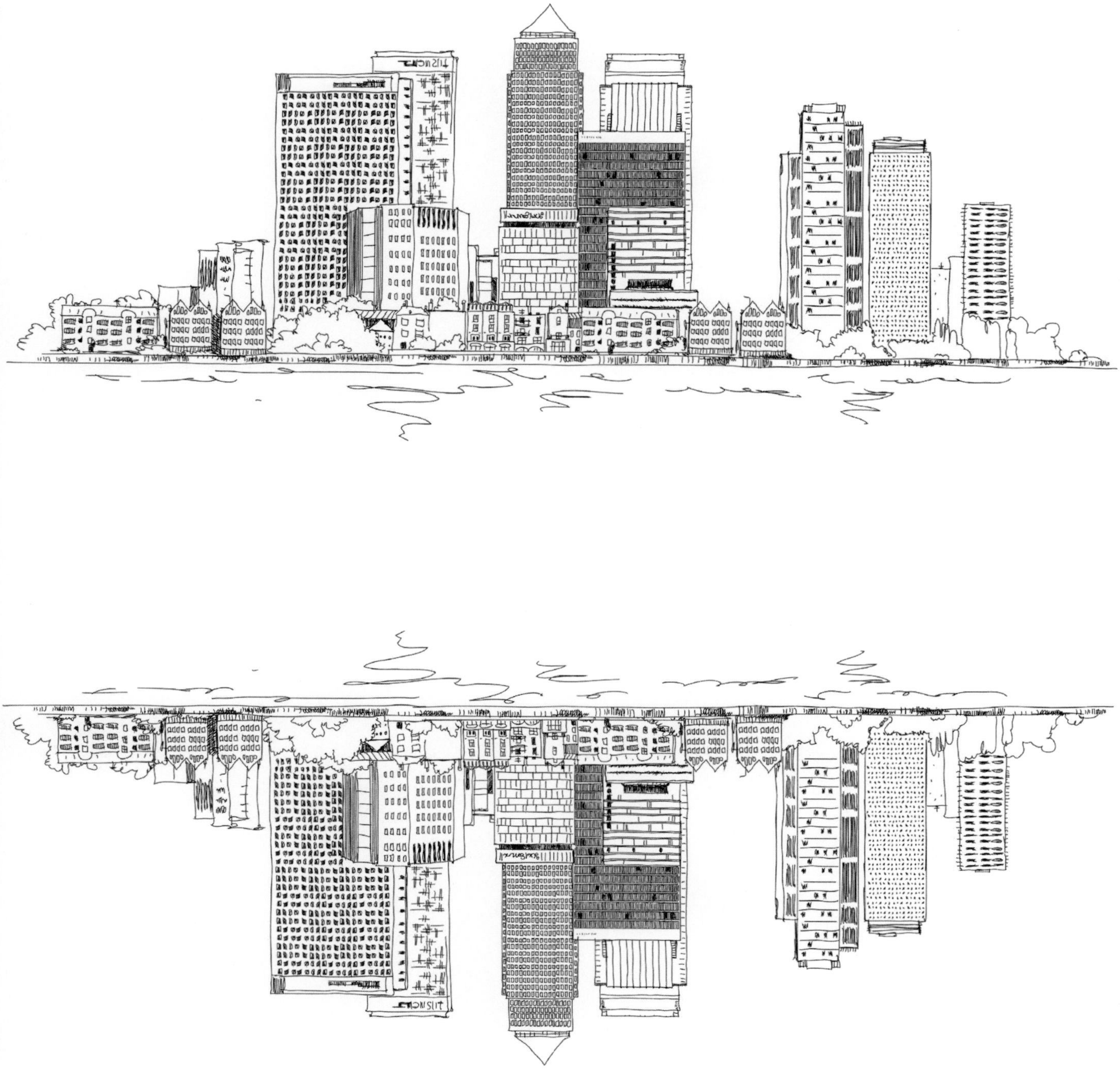

NEW YORK

# SEOUL

## KOREAN TRADITIONAL HOUSES

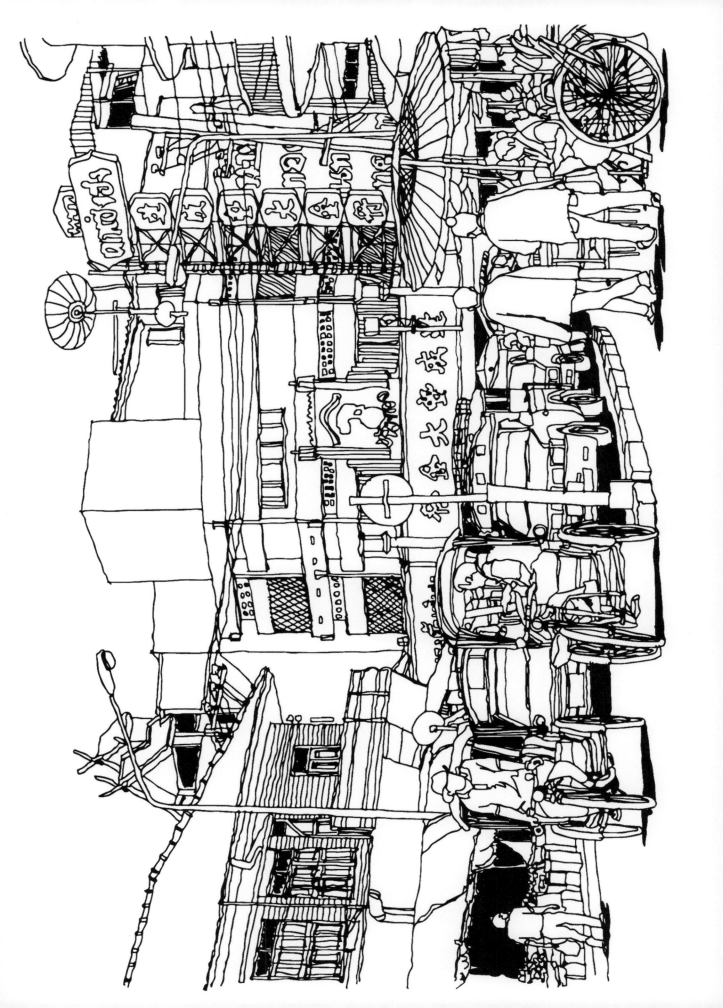

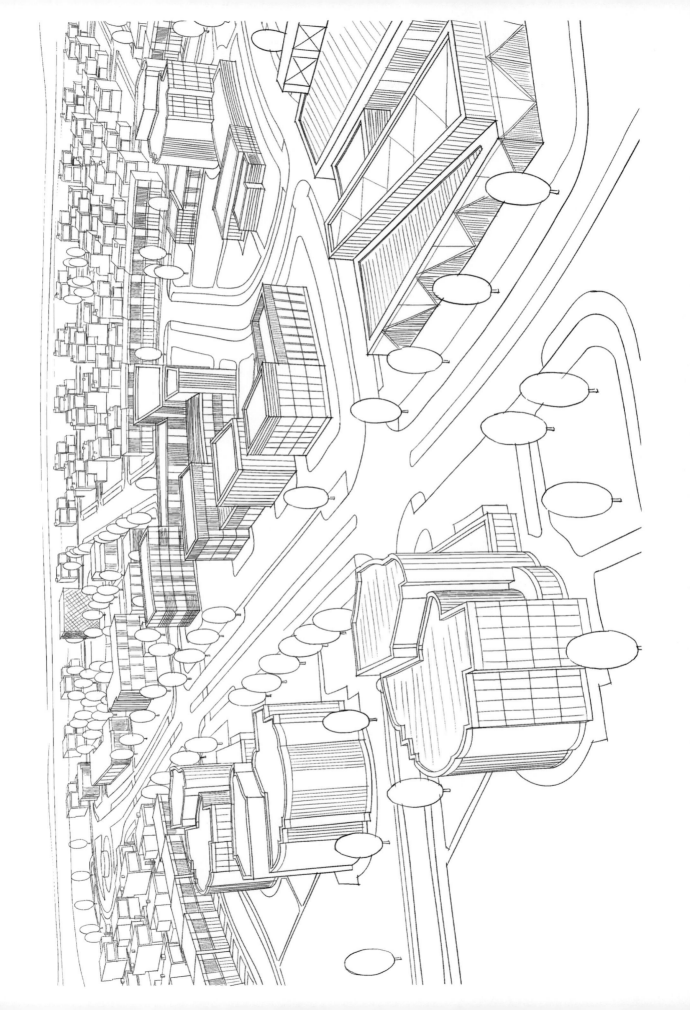

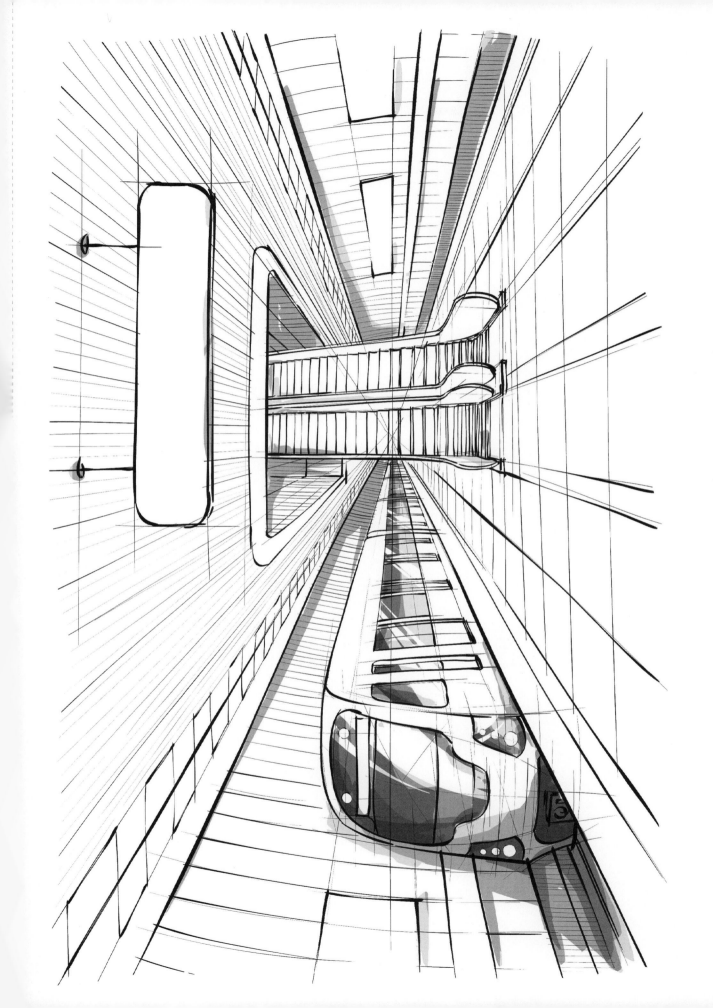

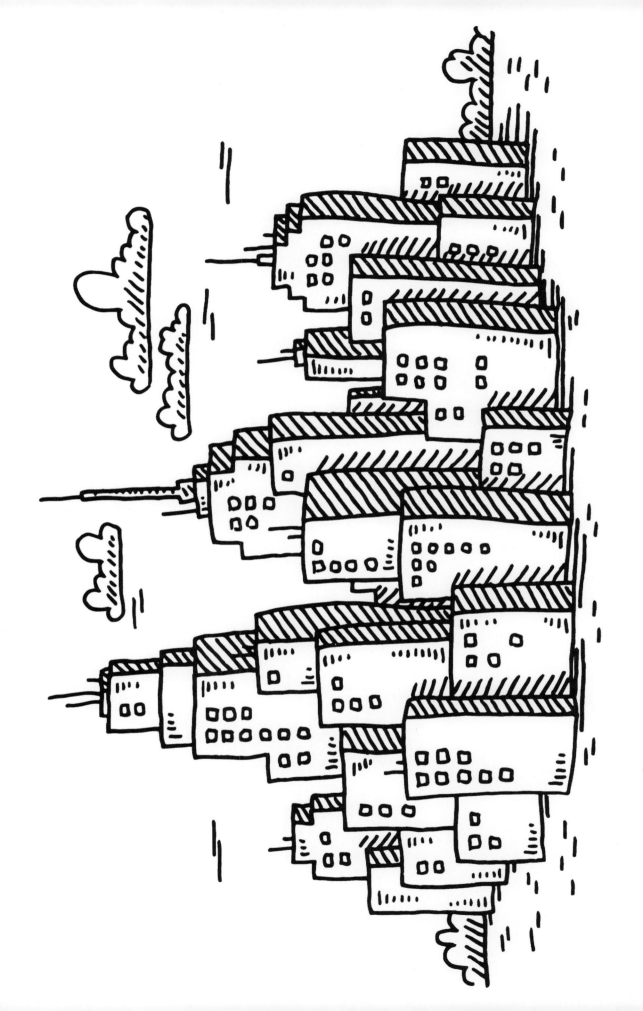

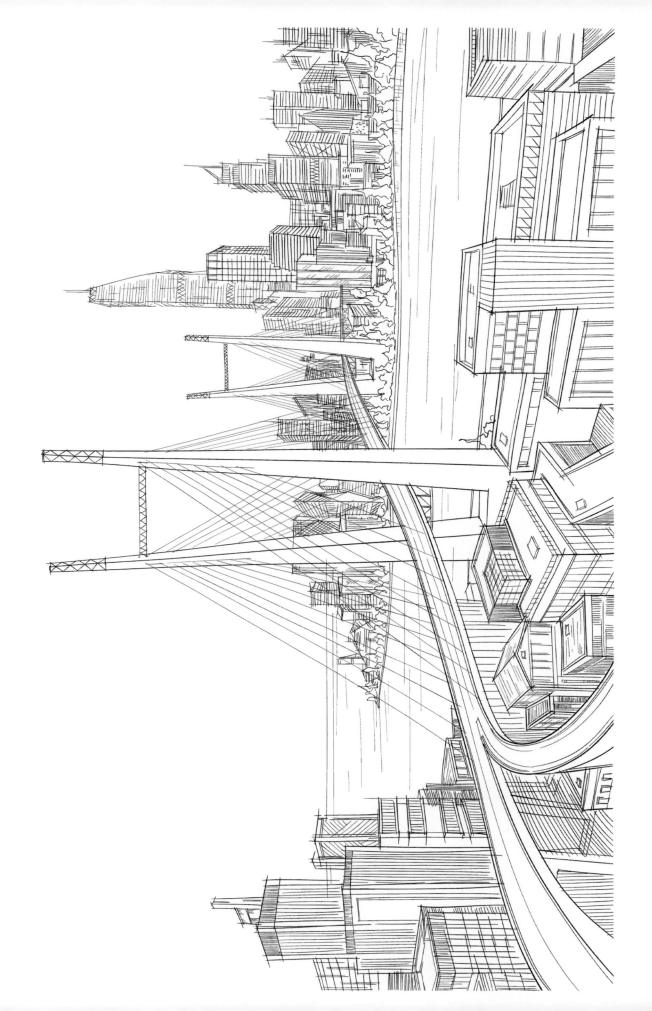

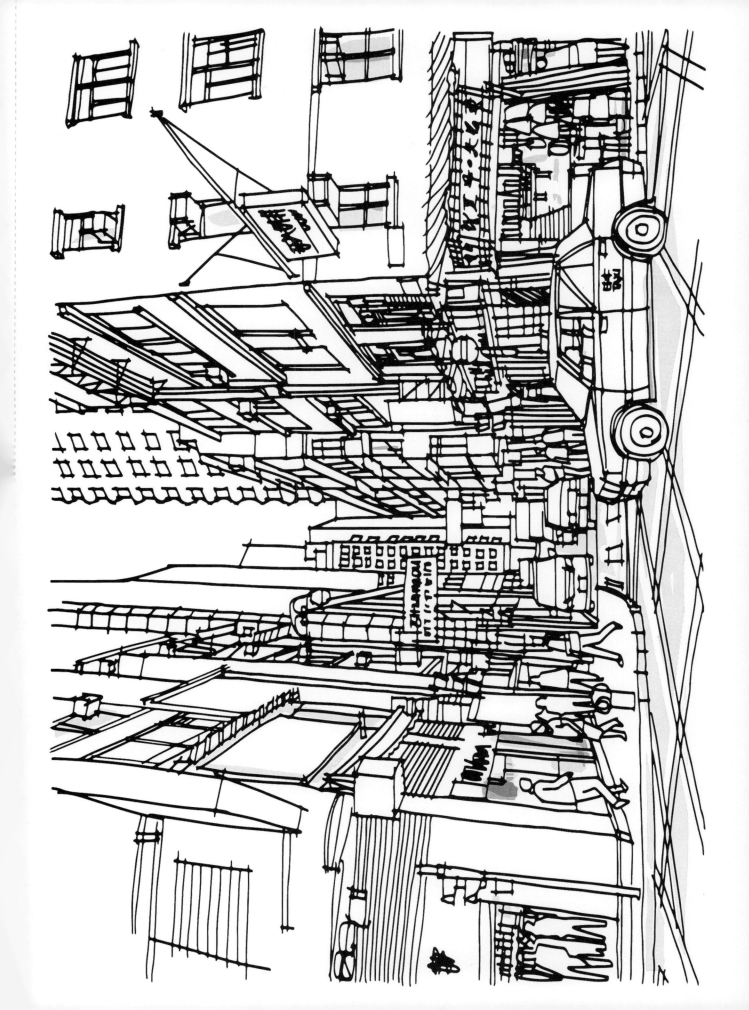

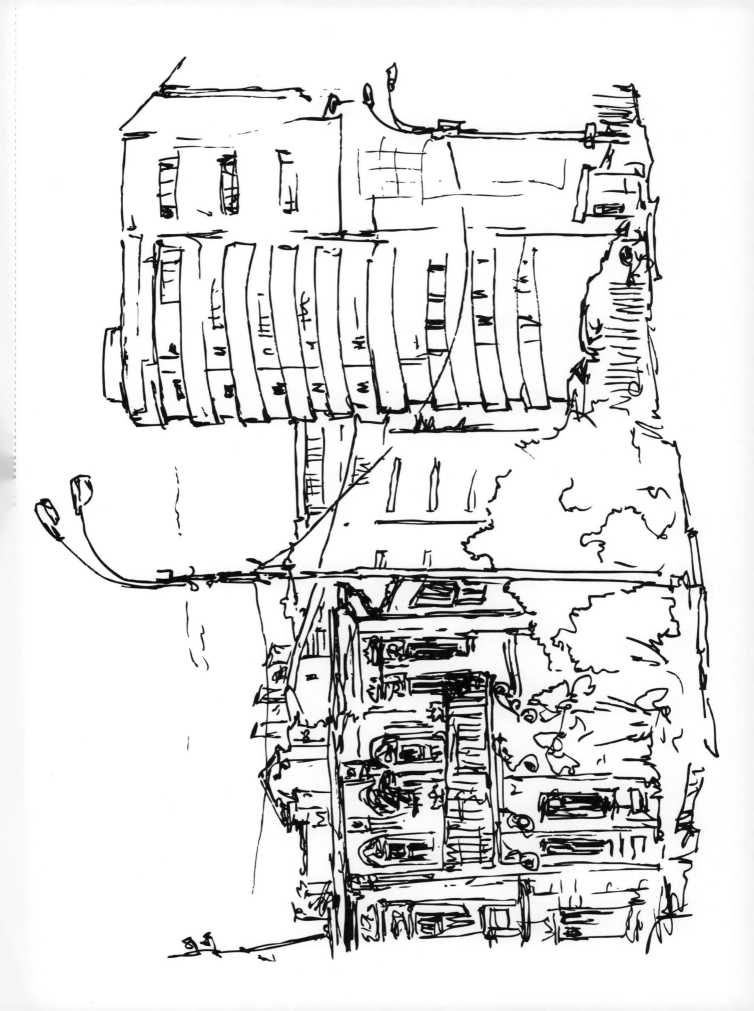

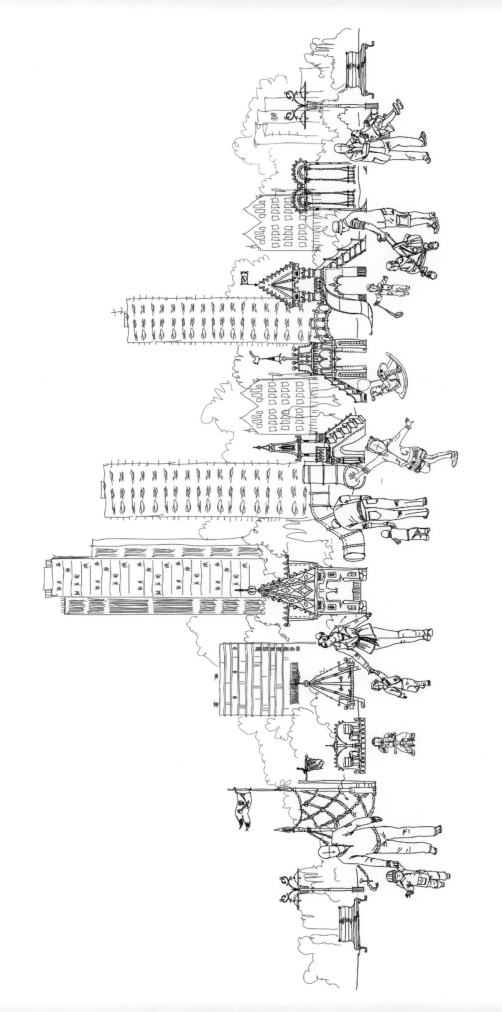

Welcome to Gold Prague

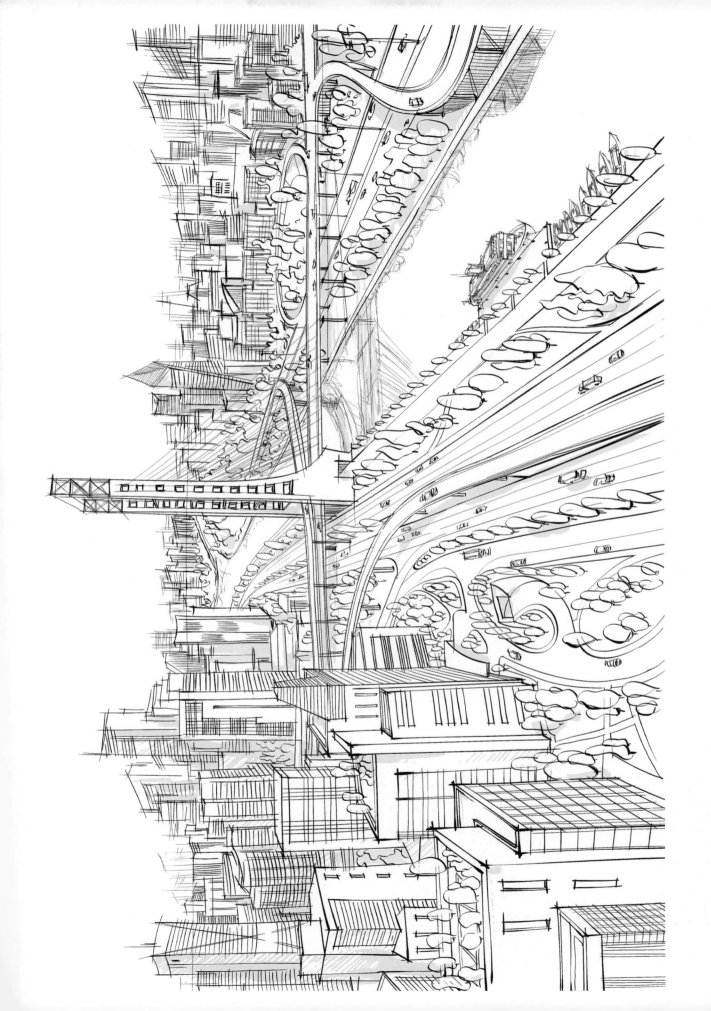

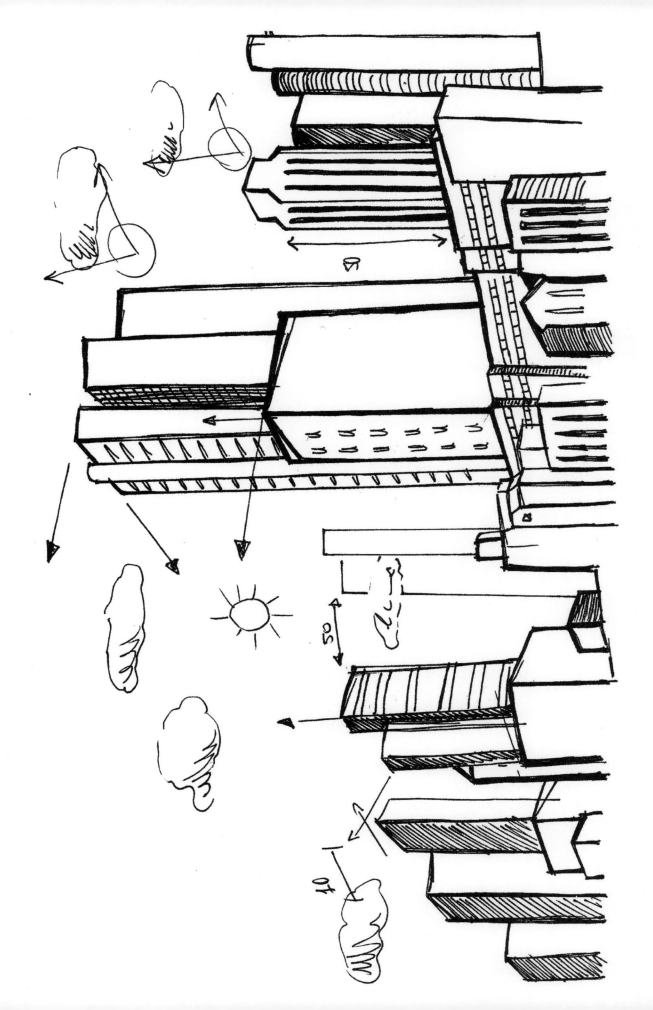

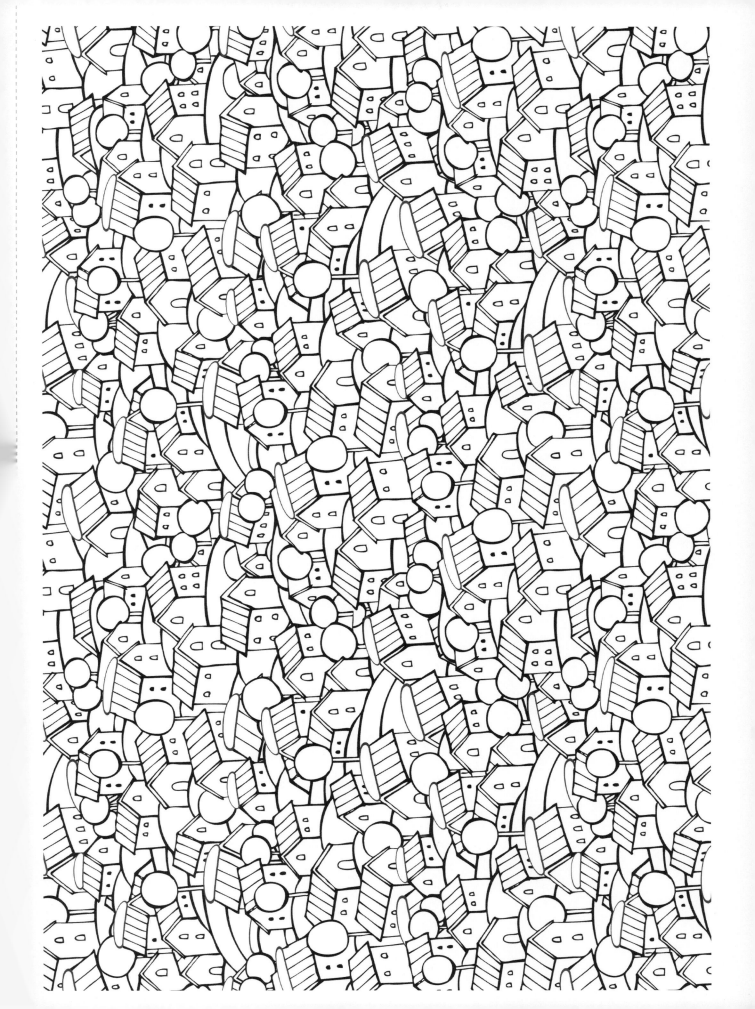

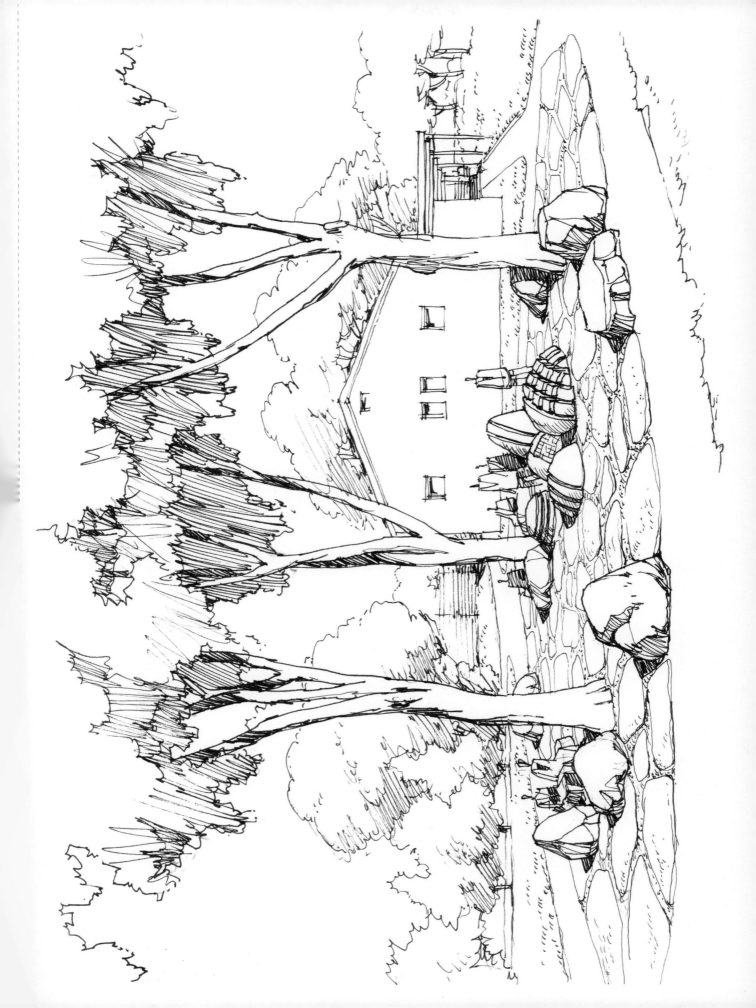

a content + ecommerce company

Other fine North Light Books are available from your favorite bookstore, art supply store or online supplier. Visit our website at fwcommunity.com.

20  19  18  17  16   5  4  3  2  1

ISBN 13: 978-1-4403-4771-9

Cover Image © iStockphoto.com/KavalenkavaVolha

Editor: Kristy Conlin
Cover Designer: Bambi Eitel
Designer: Jared Fetters
Production Coordinator: Jennifer Bass

Distributed in Canada by Fraser Direct
100 Armstrong Avenue
Georgetown, ON, Canada L7G 5S4
Tel: (905) 877-4411

Distributed in the U.K. and Europe
by F&W Media International, LTD
Brunel House, Forde Close, Newton Abbot, TQ12 4PU, UK
Tel: (+44) 1626 323200,
Fax: (+44) 1626 323319
Email: enquiries@fwmedia.com

# Ideas. Instruction. Inspiration.

Receive FREE downloadable bonus materials when you sign up for our free newsletter at artistsnetwork.com/Newsletter_Thanks.

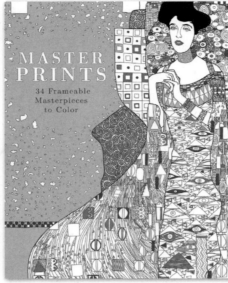

---

These and other fine North Light products are available at your favorite art & craft retailer, bookstore or online supplier.
Visit our websites: artistsnetwork.com and artistsnetwork.tv.

Follow North Light Books for the latest news, free wallpapers, free demos and chances to win FREE BOOKS!

---

# Get your art in print!

Visit artistsnetwork.com/splashwatercolor for up-to-date information on Splash and other North Light competitions.

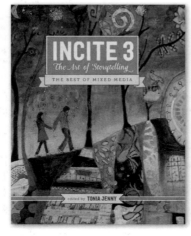